SUPER
FEMALE
SCIENTISTS™

GRACE
HOPPER

COMPUTER PIONEER

Xina M. Uhl and Christy Marx

Rosen
YA
New York

Dedicated with love to my parents: to my mother for the gift of dreams and to my father for the gift of reason

I'd like to give special thanks to Ellen Guon Beeman, Stephen Beeman, and Karen Williams for proofreading and helping me get the technical details right and to Dr. Peggy Aldrich Kidwell for sharing her time and expertise.

—Christy Marx

Published in 2020 by The Rosen Publishing Group, Inc.
29 East 21st Street, New York, NY 10010

Library of Congress Cataloging-in-Publication Data

Names: Uhl, Xina M., author. | Marx, Christy, author.
Title: Grace Hopper : computer pioneer / Xina M. Uhl and Christy Marx.
Description: New York : Rosen Publishing, 2020. | Series: Super female scientists |
Audience: Grades 7–12. | Includes bibliographical references and index.
Identifiers: LCCN 2019006750| ISBN 9781725340459 (library bound) | ISBN
9781725340442 (paperback)
Subjects: LCSH: Hopper, Grace Murray—Juvenile literature. | Women computer
engineers—United States—Biography—Juvenile literature. | Admirals—United
States—Biography—Juvenile literature.
Classification: LCC QA76.2.H67 U35 2020 | DDC 621.39092 [B]—dc23
LC record available at https://lccn.loc.gov/2019006750

Manufactured in China

On the cover: Grace Hopper, in full uniform, poses next to the US flag in 1984. She died eight years later at eighty-six years old, having lived a full and active life.

CONTENTS

INTRODUCTION

It takes a special scientist to have a US Navy guided missile destroyer named after her, but this description definitely applies to Grace Hopper. The destroyer, named the USS *Hopper*, seeks to honor Rear Admiral Hopper for her pioneering role in the development of computers. Grace Hopper's efforts in the creation of computer technology have inspired namesakes at sea and on land. The US Navy nicknamed her "Amazing Grace," but she has also been called the "Mother of Modern Naval Computing" and "Grandma COBOL."

A dedicated member of the US Navy, Hopper joined the service at thirty-seven years of age. She served her country for forty-three years, rising to the rank of rear admiral before her retirement at age eighty.

Born a mathematical genius, Hopper struggled against a male-dominated system in college, the workforce, and the military. Despite the challenges she faced, Hopper attended Yale University to earn both a master's degree and a PhD in mathematics. After graduating, she taught at Vassar College until she resigned to enter the navy's WAVES program in 1943. "WAVES" stands for "Women Accepted for Volunteer Emergency Service."

Grace Hopper poses in her office in 1984. She came from a long line of military service members, and she served in the US Navy

The following year, Hopper moved to a navy project at Harvard University, where her team developed an early prototype of the computer called the Mark I. She popularized the term "bug" to mean a software-related computer malfunction. Later achievements involved work on the first electronic digital computer, UNIVAC, and the invention of the first compiler, or a program that translates human-created instructions into codes that computers could read directly. She also codeveloped COBOL (Common Business-Oriented Language), one of the earliest standardized computer languages. In short, modern computing advancements would not have been possible without Hopper's contributions.

As a relentless advocate for technological improvements, Hopper pushed for innovative thinking, even when it bucked the existing system. A resolute woman, she never allowed obstacles to stand in her way, even those related to her gender and age.

Hopper was awarded at least thirty-seven honorary doctorates during her lifetime. These special university degrees showed her importance to the development of science, technology, engineering, and mathematics (STEM). In 1969, she received the

Man of the Year Award from the Data Processing Management Association for her contributions to computers. She went on to become the first US native—and the first woman—to be recognized as a Distinguished Fellow of the British Computer Society. The National Medal of Technology followed in 1991, and after her death, in 2016, she was granted the Presidential Medal of Freedom.

In 1994, two women scientists started the Grace Hopper Celebration, the world's largest gathering of women technologists, in honor of Hopper. The event, held yearly, attracts thousands who share new information in technology, network, and celebrate the participation of women in STEM fields. The Grace Hopper Celebration is just one way this remarkable woman scientist changed the future, and her influence continues to do so today.

CHAPTER ONE

MATURING AND MATRICULATING

The world was a different place in 1906. Horses and buggies traveled city streets alongside early automobiles. The first test flight of an airplane happened only three years prior. Silent movies played in theaters, milkmen delivered fresh milk to homes, and computers would not be invented for years to come. And also in 1906 (December 9, to be exact), a computer pioneer was born: Grace Brewster Murray, who later became Grace Hopper.

A Strong Family

Grace was born in New York City. Her mother, Mary Campbell Van Horne Murray, named Grace

This 1905 view of Broad Street in New York City shows carriages, workmen, and men in business suits congregating in the streets.

after her best friend, Grace Brewster. Mary had a deep interest in mathematics and studied geometry, but when she was a young girl, it wasn't considered proper for a young lady to study math. Her love of math was clearly passed on to her first daughter.

Grace was the oldest of her siblings. Her younger sister, Mary, was three years younger than Grace. Her brother, Roger, was five years younger. Grace's father, Walter Fletcher Murray, was an insurance broker and came from a line of builders and engineers. Walter suffered from hardening of the arteries during a time when medical treatment couldn't do much for him. When Grace entered high school, her father had to have both of his legs amputated. In spite of this, he lived to be seventy-five, getting around on wooden legs with the help of canes. He was an inspirational man who never let adversity stop him. This courage was passed on to his children.

Walter Murray was also unusual for a man of his time because he believed his daughters should have the same educational opportunities as his son, and he wanted them to spend a year working before they went to college so they would have skills with which to support themselves. With this kind of supportive

Like the girl in this photo from 1909, Grace Hopper was an active child. She did not hesitate to play with boys, but she learned how to sew as well.

family, it's no wonder Grace had the will to learn and succeed at whatever she did.

Grace was an adventurous girl who liked to climb trees, imitate cops and robbers, and play a game called kick the can. She had nontraditional toys such as construction sets and building blocks. All of the children, including Roger, were taught practical skills such as sewing, gardening, and cooking. However, Grace also learned to knit, crochet, do needlepoint, and play the piano. She loved to read, and one of her favorite books was Rudyard Kipling's *Just So Stories.*

Restless Curiosity

In the summers, the family spent time at their cottage on Lake Wentworth in Wolfeboro, New Hampshire, where Grace always had a wonderful time swimming and sailing. As a child, she was consumed with curiosity about how things worked. Author Charlene W. Billings had the good fortune to interview Grace Hopper for her book *Grace Hopper: Navy Admiral and Computer Pioneer,* in which Grace said that she could not resist a good gadget. When she was seven years old, Grace took apart an alarm clock to see how it worked, then couldn't figure out how to put it back together. She went around the cottage and took apart six more clocks before her mother caught her. Grace was confined to fiddling around with only one clock after that.

Grace told Billings the story of a moment with her father that stuck in her memory. One night in 1910, her father showed her Halley's comet. She thought

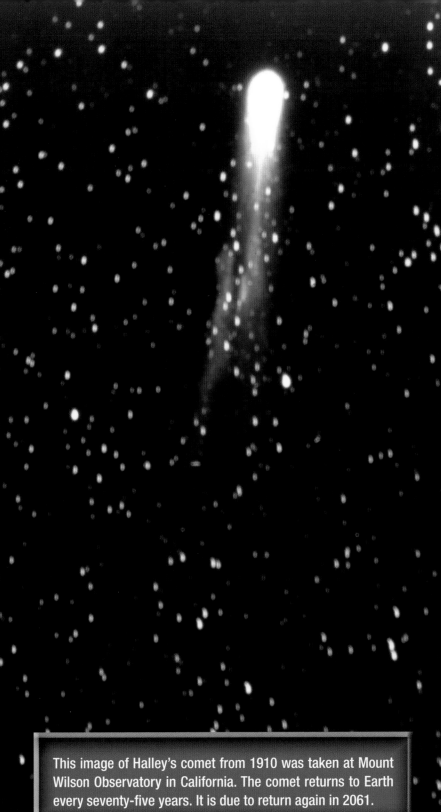

This image of Halley's comet from 1910 was taken at Mount Wilson Observatory in California. The comet returns to Earth every seventy-five years. It is due to return again in 2061.

it looked brighter than the moon. He predicted that she would live to see Halley's comet return in 1986 (and she did).

It was common for girls to be sent to private schools at the time. Grace went to Schoonmakers School, a private school in New York City that emphasized reading, history, and basic educational skills. Though girls were supposed to learn how to be ladies, Grace was able to play basketball, field hockey, and water polo. She was physically very small, but she had energy and personality to spare. Being tiny didn't stop her from taking part in sports in which her size would have been a disadvantage.

The School Years

Grace advanced quickly in school. When she was only sixteen, she applied to the prestigious Vassar College in Poughkeepsie, New York. She would have made it in at that time except that she flunked a Latin exam. She didn't like having to speak foreign languages, but she enjoyed reading them.

Vassar College made Grace wait a year before allowing her to join as a student. During that time, Grace stayed at the Hartridge School in Plainfield,

New Jersey, as a boarding student. Hartridge was an all-girls school that taught college preparatory courses. Girls were also expected to take part in singing, dancing, and other forms of exercise, such as gymnastics or calisthenics. Grace played hockey and basketball, worked on the school paper, and acted in the school plays.

Women play basketball at Vassar College in May 1913. Hopper played basketball as well as hockey while she was in college.

She graduated from Hartridge in 1924, ready to begin her college career. Next to her picture in the yearbook was this quotation by William Jennings Bryan: "In action faithful and in honor clear."

A Scientist and a Teacher

Vassar College was established in 1861 with the purpose of providing an all-women college that offered the same high educational standards as any all-male school. This was the perfect place for a bold, independent young woman like Grace Hopper. She not only took her registered courses but also added courses in all of the sciences, including botany, geology, and physiology, along with courses in economics and business. Hopper also pursued studies in mathematics and physics while keeping up with her sports activities, such as basketball. She was eager to learn, and she was a hard worker.

The teachers quickly noticed that Hopper had a talent for teaching. She was asked to tutor other students in physics, which allowed her to go beyond talking about theory by doing practical demonstrations. Throughout her career, Hopper used practical methods to bridge the gap between

KEYSTONE PUP
COPYRIGHT BY NICHOLS STUDIO 2/28/31.
NO. 4.

This photo of a Keystone Pup airplane dates from 1931. A similar plane landed at Vassar College while Hopper was a student there, causing quite a stir.

theory and reality and to help her students better understand complicated scientific terms.

She kept her adventurous spirit. Hopper remembered one day when a biplane landed near the school. She described what it was like to Billings: "Wood, linen, and wire. It had one engine and an open cockpit so you got the full benefit of the wind." Hopper decided to blow all the money she had with her—an entire ten dollars—to go up for a ride.

Switching Schools

In 1928, she graduated from Vassar College with a bachelor of arts degree in mathematics and physics. She was elected to Phi Beta Kappa, a high honor. Phi Beta Kappa is an honor society that selects members on the basis of academic achievement.

Hopper also received a grant from Vassar that allowed her to continue her education. Otherwise, she might have gone to work, since she was worried about how her parents could afford to send her sister, Mary, and her brother, Roger, to college in their turns. Mary ended up going to Vassar, and Roger followed his older sister Grace to Yale.

Hopper went to Yale University in Connecticut, where she continued her studies. Her roommate at Yale gave her a Boston terrier. Hopper had the dog for ten years.

Two years later, in 1930, she received a master's degree in mathematics and physics. That same year, at age twenty-three, she married Vincent Foster

Hopper. Grace didn't plan on becoming a traditional housewife. Instead, she managed to continue studying for her PhD at Yale by teaching at Vassar at the same time. Having an income from Vassar enabled Grace to continue her studies.

Married Life in the 1930s

On June 15, 1930, Grace Murray married Vincent Foster Hopper in the same church in which Grace's parents had been married. In fact, the same man who had performed her parents' wedding ceremony also performed Grace and Vincent's!

Vincent Hopper was a highly educated man who graduated with honors from Princeton University. He taught English and studied comparative literature at Columbia University.

Right after they married, Grace and Vincent went on a trip to Europe, visiting locations in France, England, Scotland, and Wales. Grace was especially impressed by Stonehenge, a mysterious ancient structure made of enormous standing stones, weighing many tons each, that stand in a circle on Salisbury Plain in England.

(continued on the next page)

(continued from the previous page)

The Hoppers settled in Poughkeepsie, New York, about a two-hour train ride from New York City. They owned a Model A Ford Roadster that they were too busy to wash.

Although they had a traditional, two-story home, Grace didn't plan on becoming a traditional housewife. She continued studying for her PhD at Yale and teaching at Vassar at the same time. Having that income from Vassar enabled Grace to continue her studies and eventually earn her doctorate.

This 1930 Model A Ford Roadster would have run between $500 and $1,200 brand new. Restored models can be purchased for about $20,000 today.

In the 1930s, America suffered through what is known as the Great Depression. Because of a crash in the stock market in 1929, the American economy suffered a crippling collapse. People went broke overnight and were desperate for work.

As an instructor at Vassar, Hopper earned $800 a year. That may sound like an awfully small amount of money for a yearly salary, but money went a lot farther back then. For example, a loaf of bread cost eight cents, seeing a movie cost twenty-five cents, and you could buy a new car for less than $600.

When she began as an instructor at Vassar, Hopper taught calculus, algebra, and trigonometry. Later, she added courses in analysis, theory of probability, and statistics. By the time she left Vassar in 1943, she was an associate professor.

Becoming a Doctor

Hopper completed her doctorate work at Yale in 1934 with a PhD in mathematics. This was a rare achievement in an age when men held almost all of the PhDs.

Women who studied under Hopper and went on to have brilliant careers of their own praised her for being an outstanding and vibrant teacher. She was an inspiration to them and to many others who followed. However, this academic career was

During his address to Congress a day after the December 7, 1941, Pearl Harbor bombing, President Franklin D. Roosevelt referred to the date as one "which will live in infamy."

set aside when Hopper's life was changed by the events of 1941.

On December 7, 1941, Japan staged a surprise attack on the US naval station at Pearl Harbor, in Hawaii. The damage to the navy, as well as the loss of life, was a stunning outrage. Before that, the United States had not joined in the battles of World War II, but President Franklin D. Roosevelt and Congress quickly declared war on Japan and her allies, Germany and Italy.

Hopper first heard about the attack on Pearl Harbor while she was at home grading papers and listening to the radio. Like everyone in the country, she was touched by feelings of grief, outrage, and patriotism. Suddenly, America was plunged into action as it geared up to go to war.

CHAPTER TWO

UNSTOPPABLE HOPPER

ollowing the December 7, 1941, attacks on Pearl Harbor, Vincent Hopper and Grace's brother, Roger, both joined the US Army Air Force. Grace's father worked for the Selective Service Board (which drafted men into the military services), her mother for the Ration Board (many basic supplies were rationed during the war, such as meat, sugar, and gasoline), and her sister, Mary, worked in a factory making fuses for bombs.

Grace Hopper's family had a long history of service to their country, going all the way back to the Revolutionary War. Hopper's great-grandfather on her mother's side, Alexander Wilson Russell, was a rear admiral in the navy. She could recall how impressed she was with him even at the age of three. In Billings's book, Hopper described him: "He was tall and straight, carried a black cane with a silver top on it, and had white muttonchop whiskers, which I had never seen before."

Hopper was determined to find her own way to serve her country, but when she tried to join the navy, she found nothing but obstacles. The recruiters said she was too old, although she was only thirty-four. They said she didn't meet the physical requirements. She stood 5 feet 6 inches (1.7 meters) and weighed only 105 pounds (47.7 kilograms). They required her to weigh 121 pounds (54.9 kg) for that height. Their third argument was that her occupation as a mathematics professor was

Grace Hopper poses for the camera on June 26, 1944, the day that she graduated from the Naval Reserve Midshipmen's School.

too important to the country and she was needed in the civilian sector. But none of this sat well with the unstoppable Hopper, who had nothing else holding her back: Vincent and Grace had no children and had become separated. They eventually divorced in 1945. Vincent Hopper died that same year, and Hopper never remarried.

Making WAVES

Serving in the navy became a challenge to overcome, and Grace Hopper never backed down from a challenge. She forced Vassar to give her a leave of absence from teaching by threatening to quit if she was not granted one. She managed to get a waiver to sidestep the age, height, and weight requirements. Hopper was very resourceful.

Finally, in December 1943, Grace Hopper joined the US Naval Reserve branch known as the WAVES (Women Accepted for Volunteer Emergency Service). This was how women had to join the navy at the time, because no women were allowed into the regular military. At the time, about thirty thousand to forty thousand other women had joined the WAVES.

This World War II–era poster encouraged women to join the WAVES to do their part for the war effort. Around one hundred thousand WAVES served in the US Navy during World War II.

ENLIST IN THE
WAVES

U.S. NAVY

RELEASE A MAN TO FIGHT AT SEA

Apply to your nearest
NAVY RECRUITING STATION OR OFFICE OF NAVAL OFFICER PROCUREMENT

Top of the Class

Once she was accepted, Hopper had to attend the Naval Reserve Midshipmen's School for Women in Northampton, Massachusetts. She had to pass midshipmen's school or be booted out of the navy. She found herself surrounded by young women who were the age of the students she used to teach. They were housed in an old hotel, slept on bunk beds, and had to keep all their possessions in suitcases under their bunks.

There were tough everyday requirements. The bedsheets had to be tight enough so that a quarter would bounce off them. The women had to keep their shoes shined in any kind of weather. And, of course, they had training. Every day they took orientation courses. They had to learn all about the navy: its history, customs, and regulations. They had to learn to identify types of ships, submarines, and planes accurately and instantly. They had to undergo drills and physical education. Finally, they had reading assignments at night.

It was a tough education, but Hopper graduated first in her class. Dr. Hopper became Lieutenant (junior grade) Hopper in June 1944. Upon becoming

Lieutenant Hopper, Grace took flowers to her great-grandfather's grave. According to Billings, Hopper told him, "It's all right for females to be Navy officers."

Many of the women in the WAVES did clerical and secretarial work. Fortunately, the navy recognized that Grace Hopper had much more to offer. Hopper's first assignment was with the Bureau of Ordnance Computation at the Cruft Laboratory at Harvard University. There, she was introduced to the first digital computer, the Mark I.

The Mark I was the brainchild of Dr. Howard Aiken, who conceived the device in 1937 and was able to develop it with help from Thomas Watson Sr., the founder of IBM, who later gave the machine to the navy. The Mark I completed its first successful test in January 1943.

An Amazing Machine

However, on the day in 1944 when Hopper first arrived, she knew nothing about a computing machine. Neither did anyone else outside of the top secret project. She would be only the third person to program it, making her one of the first computer programmers in the United States.

This 1944 photo shows operators of the IBM Mark I computer at Harvard University. The Mark I was designed by Howard Aiken in 1937. He was a Harvard graduate student.

Hopper's first impression of the Mark I and her first experience with Commander Howard Aiken were recorded in Billings's book. When Hopper first laid eyes on the gigantic Mark I, she thought to herself, "Gee, that's the prettiest gadget I ever saw." To Hopper, the Mark I was the first time humans built a machine with brainpower rather than manpower.

As Big as a Barn

The Mark I measured 51 feet (about 16 m) long, 8 feet (about 2.5 m) high, and 5 feet (about 1.5 m) deep. It had a four-horsepower motor. Instead of tiny, silent microchips, it used bulky mechanical relays that had to open and close to perform calculations. Imagine thirty-three hundred of these clacking away! These days, we have devices that fit in the palm of a hand that are billions of times more powerful than that huge machine.

The navy had a profound interest in the development of the Mark I. It was used for various military purposes, such as calculating angles of new navy guns to take into account crosswinds, air density, and temperature. The navy also used it for calculating the area covered by a minesweeping detector as it was towed behind a ship and for performing the first top secret mathematical simulation of the shock waves that might be produced by an atomic bomb. These were typical of the problems Hopper worked on during her tenure at Cruft Laboratory.

Commander Aiken greeted Lieutenant Hopper with some rather frightening words: "Where the hell have you been?" She thought he was referring to the weekend she had just had off to visit her parents. It turned out that he'd been waiting for her to show up the entire time she was at midshipmen's school.

Using Binary

With no choice but to plunge right in, Hopper was glad to have help from Robert Campbell and Richard Bloch, two naval officers who were of a lower rank than Hopper. The machine understood only binary code, or long lines of zeros and ones that represent specific instructions to the computer. At the time, the only way to create this code required long hours of writing instructions that had to be input by punching holes on a continuous paper tape (or later on punched cards), which the machine would read. Each line of code was a separate step in a problem that the computer would solve.

A line of code was represented by how many holes could be punched across the width of the tape. There was space for twenty-four holes, or three groups of eight holes each. These three groups per line each represented one action for the computer to perform, or three actions per line of command. It was easy to make mistakes either by misreading the numbers or by punching the wrong holes.

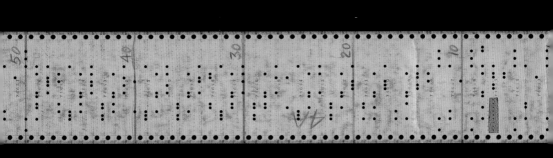

This paper machine tape is 3.6 inches (9.2 centimeters) wide. The holes punched across the width of the tape stored computerized data.

Trials and Errors

The Mark I could do calculations in one day that used to take six months to do by hand. Yet this machine, considered so amazing back then, could perform only three additions per second. The Mark I also had to be monitored twenty-four hours a day. Sometimes Hopper and her crew would have to sleep at their desks in order to be close by in case something went wrong. And things often went wrong in those early days of experimentation and discovery.

The Mark I was so big that the crew sometimes had to get inside it to find the problem. When one of its thousands of relays failed, they would track it down by the sparks it emitted. Hopper described one day when the Mark I kept shutting down every few seconds. A group of admirals chose that day to come by and see it in operation. Rather than let her staff be embarrassed, Hopper leaned against the machine and secretly kept hitting the start button. The machine made all kinds of mistakes, but the admirals didn't know any better. They thought they were seeing a perfect machine in action!

Commander Aiken proved an invaluable mentor during Lieutenant Hopper's development as a programmer. As a leader, he allowed his subordinates to make any mistake once, but if they did it again they would be in trouble.

One day, Aiken came into Hopper's office and told her that she was going to write a book. Despite her protests, she had her orders. The book was called *A Manual of Operation for the Automatic Sequence Controlled Calculator*—possibly the first ever technical manual for a computer. It was published by Harvard University.

The First Debugging

There is a story that is strongly associated with Grace Hopper that comes up just about every time someone writes about her. The story says that she is responsible for coining two of the most commonly used words in the field of computers today: "bug" (a programming error) and "debugging" (to fix programming errors).

Lieutenant Grace Hopper (*right*) and Specialist White (*left*) examine a sequence mechanism in 1944.

By 1945, the new generation of computer, the Mark II, had been built. Working conditions were not ideal, not only because Hopper and her crew had trouble finding necessary components but also because they had to rush. Their work occurred during a very hot summer. The crew had to work in an old building without air-conditioning, so they kept the windows open.

One hot day, the Mark II stopped. The crew tracked the problem down to a moth that had flown in through the open window, gotten inside the computer, and been killed by a relay opening and closing.

"We got a pair of tweezers. Very carefully, we took the moth out of the relay, put it in the logbook, and put scotch tape over it," Hopper explained. After that, whenever Commander Aiken came by and asked the team why they weren't making any progress, they would claim they were "debugging" the computer.

Hopper, however, never claimed to have invented the term "bug," because in fact she hadn't. Dr. Peggy Aldrich Kidwell oversees the mathematics collections in the Smithsonian Institution's National Museum of American History in Washington,

DC, which contains some of Hopper's personal papers and logbooks. Kidwell wrote the article "Stalking the Elusive Computer Bug," in which she researched how the word "bug" came to be used for computer problems.

Kidwell showed that using the word "bug" to mean a problem with a piece of electrical hardware goes all the way back to Thomas Edison and to telegraph operators in the 1890s. It became a word that was used by engineers to include a flaw or a problem in any apparatus, plan, or system.

The engineers at IBM who worked on the Mark I in 1944 used "bug" in this way and may well have been the ones to pass it on to Grace Hopper and her crew.

The use of "bug" obviously appealed to Hopper's quick wit and sense of humor. Among her papers are humorous drawings of imaginary "bugs" that Hopper made while working on problems with the Mark I. She drew a "table worm" that looks like a piece of the paper tape used to program the computer. She drew a caterpillar-like creature, which she called the NRL (Naval Research Laboratory) bug, and jokingly blamed it for sending the wrong data so that the machine got the wrong results. There was the "kitchie boo boo bug" that had to do with loose relays. On the same page, she drew a funny smiling face and labeled it "he who brings good data."

Obviously, Hopper was able to have fun while doing serious mathematical work. Her drawings also reveal that she and her coworkers weren't looking for physical bugs and that they used the term loosely to refer to any small problem in either the hardware (the physical machine) or the software (the program).

Then came the day (circa 1947) when they found an actual moth in the relay. After years of joking about "bugs," you can imagine how funny it must have been to them to find the real thing! It's no wonder that they took it out with such care and taped it into the logbook.

Hopper did help write glossaries of computer terms, however, and there's no doubt that she helped popularize the use of the words "bug" and "debugging" in connection with computers. Today, these are widely used words, especially in association with software. A bad piece of software is often referred to as buggy, and debugging is a vital part of completing any new program or releasing any piece of software.

CHAPTER THREE

ADVANCES ACCUMULATE

W orld War II came to an end when Germany surrendered on May 8, 1945, followed by the surrender of Japan on August 14, 1945. Grace Hopper's active duty career also ended soon after, in 1946.

Hopper wanted to transfer from the WAVES to service in the regular navy, which was allowing women to serve at that time. Once again, she was told that she was too old. She was forty, and the cutoff age was thirty-eight. She received the Naval Ordnance Development Award for her work with the Mark computer series (the Mark I and the Mark II) and was removed from active duty.

This 1944 photo shows Grace Hopper working on a manual tape punch. Using punched paper tape for data storage dates back to 1857.

She could have gone back to her teaching job at Vassar, but computers were in her blood. They were, as she put it, "more fun." She stayed on at the Harvard Computational Laboratory to help with the building of the Mark III.

The Mark Meets Business

The Mark II was five times faster than the Mark I, the Mark III was fifty times faster than the Mark II, and the Mark IV would be even faster. Already, computers were improving in vast degrees of speed. Yet they still required mathematical skill and the time-consuming coding process to turn binary code into the necessary commands.

Hopper worked at Harvard until 1949, when she took a bold step and went to work in the commercial sector. This was bold because, at the time, very few people other than Grace Hopper had a vision of what computers could become. Even IBM didn't think there would be a need for large numbers of computers or that we would eventually be using computers for business purposes. It looked as though everybody was going to settle for using punched cards forever.

The Next Thing Down the Pike

Grace Hopper knew the importance of change and often spoke of it. An article in *Chips* magazine by Elizabeth Dickason tells the story of Ginny Mullen, a retired navy commander, meeting Grace Hopper during a time when Hopper worked on computers at the Pentagon. As the story goes, Hopper would push a cart full of computer printouts from the computer workroom to her basement office. In that office, she had built something out of cardboard boxes, made to look like a television, with a picture taped to the area where the screen should be. She had labeled it "Personal Computer System." She told Mullen that "someday we would have the means of talking desk to desk, by computer."

Some of that inspiration may have come from her mentor, Howard Aiken, who envisioned a day when a computer would fill only a shoebox instead of an entire room. During Hopper's lifetime, she was able to see her predictions come true with the birth and development of personal desktop computers, the internet, and email.

But all of that lay far in the future at the time that Hopper went to work for the Eckert-Mauchly Computer Corporation in Philadelphia, Pennsylvania. She was hired as senior mathematician and remained with them until 1967.

UNIVAC Debuts

The first attempt at a mass-produced, commercial computer took place in 1951. It was called UNIVAC I (Universal Automatic Computer). Instead of using punch cards, it used high-speed magnetic tape to record data. It was only 14.5 feet (about 4.5 m) long, 9 feet (about 3 m) wide, and 7.5 feet (about 2 m) tall—far smaller than earlier computers, and far, far faster.

The coding Hopper was doing on these machines was based on the mathematical system known as octal. It uses a total of eight digits, starting with 0 and ending with 7. She had to teach herself to do all her math—adding, subtracting, multiplying, and dividing—in octal, a numbering system that uses eight, rather than ten, as a base. She got very good at this, maybe a little too good. Pretty soon, she began to have trouble balancing her checkbook. Her brother, Roger, then a banker, went through her accounts and discovered that every once in a while, she'd use octal math instead of regular ten-digit math.

Inventing ENIAC

J. Presper Eckert and John Mauchly had been developing their own electronic computers during the war. The first was known as ENIAC (Electronic Numerical Integrator and Calculator). Like the Mark series, it was huge, more than 100 feet (about 30 m) long and 10 feet (about 3 m) high, contained more than 18,000 glass electronic vacuum tubes, and weighed more than 30 tons (27.2 metric tons). But instead of using mechanical devices

These female computer operators in 1940 are plugging and unplugging cables and flipping switches on the first electronic digital computer, ENIAC.

such as levers, it used electrical pulses and had almost no moving parts.

Next they developed EDVAC (Electronic Discrete Variable Automatic Computer). It was faster and included other advances, such as being able to keep the instructions for a calculation in its memory instead of requiring external input.

When Hopper went to work with Eckert and Mauchly, they were just completing BINAC (Binary Automatic Computer). One of Hopper's jobs was to teach the people at Northrop Aircraft Corporation how to use it.

The Eckert-Mauchly Computer Corporation was eventually bought by Remington Rand, which then merged into the Sperry Corporation, now known as UNISYS.

A Different Kind of Language

During this time, Hopper became convinced that it would be possible to teach a computer to write its own programs. She knew there needed to be a way for ordinary people, rather than mathematicians who could do octal math, to tell a computer what to do. What was needed was a programming language that anybody could understand.

In 1952, Hopper developed the A-0 System ("A" stands for "algebraic," and "0" was the first version). It was the first compiler. A compiler is a way to translate mathematical symbols that humans can read into machine code that a computer can understand. Hopper had collected pieces of mathematical code, or routines, that were used over and over again in many different programs. Next, she gave each of these routines a call number. Then she could simply use the call number and that routine would be pulled from where it was stored on the magnetic tape and put into use. Once she wrote down a set of call numbers, the computer found them on tape. Then she brought them over and did the additions.

Compiling a Compiler

Hopper used an unusual source of inspiration to solve one of the problems she had in creating the A-0 compiler—her experience playing basketball. Back when Hopper had been playing basketball, the rules allowed a woman to dribble only once, then not take another step, so to keep the ball moving forward she would have to throw a forward pass to another teammate. Then she would run to a new forward position and her teammate would throw the ball back to her.

She applied that to the compiler by identifying a section at the end of the memory that she labeled a "neutral corner." When she wanted to jump forward out of the routine she was working on, she jumped to a spot in the "neutral corner." Next, she set up a flag for an operation that alerted her that she had a message. The message meant that each routine had to look and see if it had a flag. If the routine found a flag, it put a second jump from the neutral corner to the routine's beginning.

It is difficult to convey just what a radical change in thinking and design the compiler was in the world of computers. It was the beginning of what we know as modern computer programs and was possibly Grace Hopper's greatest contribution to the development of computer software. It paved the way for everything that was to follow in the development of user-friendly computers. Every piece of software today, from spreadsheets to console games, relies on the use of compilers. Even the word "flag" is sometimes still used in computer programming to indicate something the computer is supposed to catch and do in response to the action of the user.

Creating FLOW-MATIC

Hopper didn't stop there. The A-0 evolved into the A-1 and the A-2 as she kept improving it. Yet it took Hopper years to overcome industry skeptics and convince people of what her compiler could do.

Sometime around 1950, Charles H. Doersam Jr. was part of a small group of computer people, and Hopper was the only woman in the group. In an article by Gordon R. Nagler for the National Academy of Engineering, Doersam related how Hopper created quite a stir by getting up and telling them that she had heard enough from the men about their fine hardware, and now they needed to listen while she described her "software."

Hopper had the idea that computer programs could be written in English. She didn't see why the letters of the alphabet couldn't be translated into machine code the same as numbers and mathematical symbols.

In typically modest fashion, Hopper claimed that no one thought of it before her because she was lazier than most people. She didn't want to spend all that time writing difficult code, she just wanted to get the work done. With that in mind, she developed the B-0 compiler ("B" standing for "business"), but it's probably better known for the name it acquired later, the FLOW-MATIC. It was specifically designed to handle business procedures such as payroll and billing.

It was a huge accomplishment when she was able to teach UNIVAC to read twenty written commands by 1956. The kind of words used by the FLOW-MATIC were add, multiply, subtract, divide, count, move, and replace.

Hopper was so far ahead of her time that she could see how the FLOW-MATIC would be adapted to other languages besides English. As usual, nobody wanted to believe her. They would say critical things, such as claiming that an American computer built in Philadelphia, Pennsylvania, couldn't understand French or German.

CHAPTER FOUR

NEW OPPORTUNITIES AND NANOSECONDS

I n the mid-1950s, other companies were starting to follow suit by developing early programming languages such as FORTRAN (FORmula TRANslation), devised by IBM. None of them used English commands the way the FLOW-MATIC did. Furthermore, none of these languages were compatible with other machines. One type of programming language could be used with only one type of computer. There was no standard way to do things.

Finally, in 1959, a technical committee was formed that represented big business interests, the military, and the largest of the business

This Boston, Massachusetts, computer instructor teaches a 1968 class on the FORTRAN computer language, an early programming language.

machine manufacturers. They came up with a recommendation that had nothing to do with the programming languages developed by either IBM or UNIVAC. They called what they came up with COBOL (COmmon Business Oriented Language). But there were a couple of problems. For one thing, their attempt to create a COBOL language didn't work. Second, IBM refused to accept it, and it would never get anywhere without agreement from IBM. Now the race was on for someone to come up with a version of COBOL that everyone would accept.

In 1960, Grace Hopper demonstrated a version of COBOL that would run on both UNIVAC and RCA computers. It was another two years before IBM finally accepted using COBOL as a standard language.

An Acknowledged Expert

A European committee began to work with the American committee toward standardizing COBOL on a more global basis. Over the years, COBOL continued to grow and develop until it became the basis of nearly every computer program in the world. It was used to process large volumes of data and was utilized for things such as payroll, inventory, and accounting. The kind of basic words COBOL could process included run, move, get, add, multiply, divide, transfer, and stop. It is still widely in use today.

Hopper was acknowledged as one of the vital forces in creating COBOL. It was thanks to her vision and foresight that the language was written using easily understood English commands, in spite of unimaginative people telling her it couldn't be done.

This is one of the most significant changes in the history of computer evolution, and she won awards for it. In 1969, she was named the first-ever Computer Science Man of the Year by the Data Processing Management Association (although she was surely not a man!). In 1973, she became a Distinguished Fellow of the British Computer Society. By doing so, she became the first person from the United States and the first woman of any nationality to win this prestigious prize.

And there were many, many more awards earned during her lifetime. You'd think this was enough for most people, but Grace Hopper was just getting started.

In 1966, Hopper received a letter from the navy reminding her that she had served in the Naval Reserves for twenty-three years. It also reminded her that she was sixty years old. Then she read on and realized that the letter was actually asking her to apply for retirement. Hopper was saddened, but she retired from the reserves with the rank of commander. This retirement lasted for only seven months.

This portrait of Grace Hopper was taken in 1965. The prior year, Hopper was honored with Achievement Awards from the Society of Women Engineers.

A new federal law gave the National Bureau of Standards the responsibility of overseeing the standardization of COBOL, and the man who had to do that job was Norman Ream, who had previously worked for the secretary of the navy. The navy was unable to develop a working payroll plan after 823 attempts. Ream needed help, and he called for Commander Grace Hopper. It was supposed to be a temporary assignment of six months, but it lasted for almost twenty years.

Hopper was assigned a room in the Pentagon and was given a small staff to help her. What they didn't do was provide her with furnishings. Hopper had to buy herself a coffeepot for her office. She and her staff came in at night and helped themselves to some furniture from other offices. When someone complained about the missing furniture, her defense was to say it was not bolted down.

Grace Hopper had a couple of other items that were unusual to find in a navy commander's office. She had a skull and crossbones pirate flag, a sure sign of her independent personality. And she had a clock that ran backward (counterclockwise). Hopper kept this clock as a visual reminder to herself or anyone else that the words she hated to hear most were,

$20,000 or Bust

According to Billings, Hopper once had to give a presentation to the secretary of the navy and other high-ranking officials. A navy captain (a higher rank than her rank as commander) was escorting her to the room where she'd have to give her speech. The captain told her that she would be the first woman to give a presentation in that room. That didn't do much to put Hopper at ease. Then he told her that it would also be the first time anyone below the rank of captain had given a presentation in that room. She was rattled by the time she entered the room.

She gave her speech, and afterward the secretary of the navy asked if there was anything she needed. Rather than being at all intimidated by the man to whom she was talking, Hopper promptly asked for a larger staff and $20,000 to conduct a survey to find out what COBOL users needed.

He promised to do what he could, and then the room collapsed into laughter. Hopper fled outside and asked the navy captain what on earth she had done. He said, "Don't you realize that no one ever asks for less than twenty million dollars in that room?"

"We've always done it that way." This clock was a prime example of a different but equally valid way of doing things. It seems odd only because we're not used to it. Elizabeth Dickason said that Hopper's message was this: Be innovative, be open minded, and give people the freedom to try new things.

A New Title

Commander Hopper's position was director, Navy Programming Languages Group, Office of Information Systems Planning and Development. Her title was quite a mouthful.

Here, she was basically doing what she had been doing for years—finding ways to standardize the development of COBOL so that the system would work for all kinds of computers and programs and making sure that COBOL was used throughout the navy.

In 1973, Hopper was promoted to the rank of captain. This was also the year she was awarded the Legion of Merit, a special award created by Congress in 1942, given for the performance of outstanding services by military personnel.

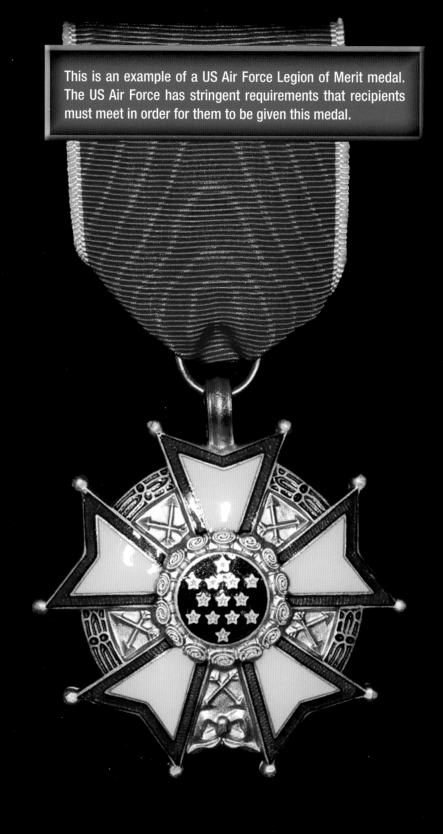

This is an example of a US Air Force Legion of Merit medal. The US Air Force has stringent requirements that recipients must meet in order for them to be given this medal.

Hopper remained in the navy for decades, but during that time she did far more than mathematical calculations and computer programming. One of the things she did best was teach, and she'd been doing that ever since she was a graduate student at Vassar.

No matter what else she was doing, whether she was working at a private company or for the navy, Hopper traveled to teach and give lectures. She served as visiting lecturer or visiting associate professor at various engineering schools, including the ones at the University of Pennsylvania and George Washington University in Washington, DC.

Hopper didn't keep the money she received from her speaking engagements. Instead, she donated it—a total of $114,295—to the Navy Relief Society for financial and educational help to members of the navy and their families.

Divisions of Time

Hopper was an excellent speaker who knew how to explain things in a way that was easy to understand. One of the examples for which she is especially well remembered was her explanation of the nanosecond.

As computers became faster and faster, Hopper wrestled with understanding tinier and tinier units of time. Even though she knew the definition of a millisecond (one-thousandth of a second), it was still hard for her to understand it fully. Her frustration grew when she then tried to understand a microsecond (one-millionth of a second), a nanosecond (one-billionth of a second), and a picosecond (one-trillionth of a second).

Hopper became so frustrated with trying to grasp these units that she made a call to some engineers and asked them to send her a nanosecond. She was probably just being funny, but the engineers took her seriously. Or at least they came up with a more or less serious way of answering her. They sent her a piece of wire that was 11.78 inches (about 30 cm) long. This piece of wire represented how far electricity could go through the wire in the span of a nanosecond.

Hopper was delighted. Next, she asked for a piece of wire that would represent the length of a microsecond (a mere one-millionth of a second). This piece of wire was an entire coil that was 984 feet (about 300 m) long!

Grace Hopper distributed a nanosecond bundle in the late 1960s to demonstrate how smaller components like these would decrease computer processing times.

Remember how the Mark I was thought to be so fast because it could do three operations per second? One operation can be getting a value out of memory, storing another value in memory, or adding one value to another, and so on. Now we have memory chips that can do *billions* of operations per second, meaning more than one operation per nanosecond.

An admiral once asked Hopper to explain why it took so long for a message to be sent by satellite. Hopper pointed the nanosecond piece of wire toward space and explained to him that there were many nanoseconds between where they were and the satellite.

Permission or Apology?

Hopper would bring the nanosecond piece of wire and the microsecond coil of wire to the hundreds of lectures she gave, and they were always a big hit. Her lectures would be packed to overflowing, and afterward people would line up to receive one of Hopper's nanoseconds, which she would hand out.

As a speaker, Hopper had a particular talent for radiating energy and enthusiasm to captivate her audience. She was remembered for her simple but powerful philosophy of courage and boldness that boiled down to "If it's not bolted down (you can take it)" and "It's easier to ask forgiveness than to get permission." To illustrate what she meant by these sayings, Hopper had a variety of stories she would rely on to explain them.

One story involved a young navy lieutenant who served on a small ship. The navy thought the ship was too small to have a computer. The lieutenant didn't agree, though, and he brought his own computer with him and put all the ship's records into it. He was so efficient that when he left, the captain had to buy the computer from him to keep the ship running properly.

In another version of the story, a sailor built a computer on a ship. This initiative brought him to the attention of a rear admiral. Eventually, the sailor ended up working for NARDAC (Navy Regional Data Automation Center) and took part in creating the first microcomputer conference.

Another version of the story was about a young navy officer who used a computer to maintain the records for his aircraft carrier–based plane while at sea. He would stow the computer behind the seat of his plane. He mentioned it later, and someone asked, "Were you supposed to do that?" "I didn't ask," the officer replied.

The submarine control room of the USS *Nautilus* shows how cramped such quarters would be. In such cases, smaller, more powerful computers are quite helpful.

Whichever version might be correct (or even if all three of them are), they contain the same basic kernel of truth that Hopper wanted to communicate: it's easier to ask forgiveness than it is to get permission. In other words, when she saw something that needed to be done to achieve a goal, and she knew people without the necessary vision or foresight would stand in her way, she would go ahead and do what needed to be done and worry about being forgiven for it later. Of course, the trick is to do something that proves to be so worthwhile that you don't have to worry about being forgiven. This was the way Hopper got things done and how she advised others to get things done, too.

CHAPTER FIVE

MOVING ON AHEAD

The tireless Hopper was extraordinarily busy when she was in her seventies, an age when most people are sitting back and taking it easy. In 1982, Hopper went to give a lecture to the students at Brewster Academy in Wolfeboro, New Hampshire. Wolfeboro was the area where she spent those adventurous summers of her youth, a place she remembered fondly.

At this academy, she spoke about computers and visited two classes that taught COBOL programming. Both Hopper and the staff of the academy were enthusiastic about the idea of establishing a computer center for the school. She

Commodore Grace Hopper speaks at a groundbreaking ceremony for the Grace M. Hopper Regional Data Automation Center in North Island, California, on September 27, 1985.

used her many contacts within the industry to help make this happen. She turned to people at large corporations such as Wang, Digital Equipment Corporation, and 150 other businesses, convincing them to support the creation of the center.

About a year later, in November 1983, the academy was able to open the Grace Murray Hopper Center for Computer Learning. The governor of New Hampshire declared November 7 Captain Grace Murray Hopper Day.

A Marvelous Mentor

In addition to being energetic and dedicated, Hopper was a warm, generous woman. Ginny

Mullen, a retired navy commander, told a story of Hopper's keen memory and thoughtfulness, which was published on the US Navy's *Chips* website.

It was a day when Mullen was relating how she had gotten into the navy. "I told her of having a godmother who had been a Radioman WAVE during WWII [World War II] and about the paper doll book I had been given." The next time Mullen ran into Hopper, Hopper presented her with a book of WAVE and marine women paper dolls. It was the kind of gesture that made Grace Hopper a valued mentor to so many young people.

Promotions

The rank of captain was only a stop along the way to Hopper's advancement in the navy. On December 15, 1983, she was promoted to the rank of commodore. At the time, Hopper was seventy-six, and she was considered too old to be eligible for promotion. Because it couldn't be done in the normal way, Representative Philip Crane introduced a bill into Congress to make it happen. He believed that it was time for Hopper to be honored and recognized for her outstanding work. He became inspired to

Hopper's Truisms

Grace Hopper was known for her colorful quotes. Here are a few examples, compiled by Philip Scheiber for the *OCLC Newsletter* (Online Computer Library Center):

- "You manage things, you lead people."
- "We're flooding people with information. A human must turn information into intelligence or knowledge. We've tended to forget that no computer will ever ask a new question."
- "In pioneer days, they used oxen for heavy pulling, and when one ox couldn't budge a log, they didn't try to grow a larger ox. We shouldn't be trying for bigger computers, but for more systems of computers."

do this after seeing Hopper on television doing an interview for the news show *60 Minutes*. The bill was approved, and Hopper received her promotion by special presidential appointment from President Ronald Reagan.

Two years later, in 1985, she was promoted once again to rear admiral. When she received that historic promotion, she was only the seventh woman ever to become a rear admiral in the US Navy. According to Billings, she joked to some friends that her great-grandfather, the one who had been a rear admiral himself, might actually rise from the dead at the news.

It was in September 1985 that NARDAC (Navy Regional Data Automation Center) began building a new facility in San Diego, California (now known as the Naval Computer and Telecommunications Station). It was dedicated as the Grace Murray Hopper Service Center. The purpose of this center was to contain a data processing center and to provide training facilities, teleconferencing and telecommunications capabilities, and the Grace Hopper Museum to display many of her awards, military decorations, and university degrees.

Hopper loved to wear her uniform and would laugh over the way people misinterpreted who she was. She was mistaken for a flight attendant and once for a security guard. People were often surprised that someone of her age could still be in the navy. Time and again, Hopper had been told she was too old or that she needed to retire.

A Conference with *Chips*

One of Admiral Hopper's other great areas of enthusiasm was the Navy Micro Conference, which began in 1982. Hopper would give the keynote speech during the early years, as it grew from a small conference of about four hundred people to a conference attended by thousands who came to exchange the latest information on computers. This conference is now known as Connecting Technology, and it takes place twice a year, once on the East Coast and once on the West Coast.

Along with giving the Micro Conference, NARDAC in Norfolk, Virginia, began publishing a newsletter called *Chips Ahoy*, which is now just called *Chips* magazine. Their founding motto is "Dedicated to Sharing Information, Technology and Experience."

Grace Hopper had a strong feeling about *Chips*. Diane Hamblen, who began editing the magazine in 1986, recalls with great humor her first meeting with the legendary Hopper in a memorial editorial she wrote for the April 1992 issue of *Chips*.

Hamblen decided to start her *Chips* career "with a bang" by interviewing Grace Hopper. She made the phone calls, and a meeting was arranged for a Wednesday night at nine o'clock, during one of the Micro Conferences. "Swell," Hamblen thought. "That's past my bedtime, and I was absolutely certain it was past lights out for a 70-year-old-plus, admiral or not."

At the appointed time, Hamblen showed up with her tape recorder, spare tapes, pen and paper, and list of questions. Exactly at nine o'clock, Admiral Hopper showed up at the lobby of the hotel. She walked up to Hamblen, shook her hand, and said, "So you're the new *Chips* editor. What makes you think you can do the job?"

From this daunting start, Hamblen began the interview. "But it sure established who controlled who. We talked; I asked my questions. She talked; I changed tapes. She talked some more; I changed tapes again. I ran out of tape. She was winding up; I was winding down."

Hamblen admits that by 10:45 p.m., it was way past her bedtime and she was sagging, but by that time, Hopper had gathered an audience of interested listeners. At midnight, she said, "I tottered to my car, leaving her still holding court with her fan club."

The next morning, Hamblen was at work when her boss rushed up in a panic. "Admiral Hopper wants to see you. You left last night before she was finished."

That is how Hamblen found herself towed around the convention center behind the diminutive admiral, with Hopper "all the while lecturing me on what she expected from *Chips*."

Moving On

On August 14, 1986, at the age of seventy-nine, Grace Hopper retired from the navy for the final time. She asked to have her retirement ceremony take place on the deck of a famous ship, the USS *Constitution*, also known as Old Ironsides. She must have felt something in common with the ship: It was the oldest commissioned warship still in use, and when she retired she was the oldest commissioned officer on active duty.

It was a huge ceremony with full honors attended by about three hundred people: friends, navy officials, dignitaries, people who had worked with her in World War II, and members of her family.

The secretary of the navy, John F. Lehman Jr., gave her the Distinguished Service Medal of the Department of Defense, which he pinned onto her

Navy secretary John F. Lehman Jr. honors Admiral Grace Hopper during her retirement ceremony aboard the USS *Constitution* on August 14, 1986, in Boston, Massachusetts.

uniform. It is the Defense Department's second-highest honor that can be awarded.

As reported by Richard Pearson for the *Washington Post*, on January 4, 1992, Lehman told this joke: "I'm reminded of that famous story by P. T. Barnum. About the turn of the century, his principle attraction, the human cannonball, came to P. T. Barnum and said, 'Mr. Barnum, I just can't take it any longer. Two performances a day and four on weekends are just too much. I'm quitting.' Barnum said, 'You can't possibly quit. Where will I find someone else of your caliber?'"

He also said of Hopper: "She's challenged at every turn the dictates of mindless bureaucracy." He recalled, "[Once Hopper] gave me a stern lecture on computers. It was the roughest wire brushing I've had since I got this job."

There were more speeches made, a printed citation was handed out, a navy band played patriotic songs, sailors cheered, and Hopper was given forty-three long-stemmed roses to signify her forty-three years of service to the navy.

This time, Admiral Hopper had truly retired, right? Not exactly.

A LEGEND'S LEGACY

Though she retired from the navy, Grace Hopper didn't slow down. In fact, she joined the Digital Equipment Corporation (DEC) as a senior consultant. There, she represented the organization by working with schools and giving presentations on advanced computing concepts and the importance of information and data.

For the next four years or so, she did lecture tours around the country at colleges, universities, and engineering forums. She continued to receive awards. In September 1991, when Hopper was eighty-four, she received the National Medal of Technology. This is the United States' highest honor in engineering and technology, and Grace

Forty high school students attend the 2013 Anita Borg Institute's Grace Hopper Celebration of Women in Computing.

Hopper was the first woman individually recognized with the award.

In fact, at the end of her life, she had two apartments—one that she lived in and one that was overflowing with her papers and memorabilia. One room alone was filled entirely with plaques she had received over the decades.

Awards and More Awards

In addition to the huge number of awards Dr. Hopper received during her life, there are numerous awards that have been named in her honor. Here are some of them:

- The Grace Murray Hopper Award for Outstanding Young Scientist: This prestigious award is given by the Association for Computing Machinery.
- The Grace Hopper Award for Computing and Grace Hopper Scholarships: This award is given by the Grace Hopper Celebration of Women in Computing, an annual technical conference.
- The Grace Hopper Government Technology Leadership Awards (also known as the Gracies): These are given out by the United States General Services Administration.
- The Grace Hopper Memorial Award: This is a scholarship in computer science given by Bowling Green State University in Ohio.
- The Grace Hopper Lecture Series: This is run each year by the University of Pennsylvania's School of Engineering and Applied Science. It is intended to serve the dual purpose of recognizing successful women in engineering and inspiring students to achieve at the highest level.

- Rear Admiral Grace Hopper Cup: This prize is awarded by the Arizona Civil Air Patrol to the "Arizona launch-team member who demonstrates innovative leadership solutions and the ability to think 'outside the box.'"

Possibilities of the Future

From beginning to end, Hopper was a visionary. She saw the potential for computers to do things such as track the life cycle of crop-eating locusts, track waves at the bottom of the ocean, run all the electrical systems in a house, handle family bookkeeping and accounts, manage water reserves to guarantee a fair distribution of water, and perform weather prediction on a global scale. She even foresaw more radical changes in computers when they might be powered by bursts of light instead of electricity.

Hopper was especially concerned about weather prediction and water usage. She looked ahead to the importance of how climate changes would affect the planet, and she anticipated how the continuously increasing population will find itself competing more and more for limited water sources.

This 2001 photo, taken by the crew of the space shuttle *Atlantis*, shows Destiny, the US laboratory on the International Space Station in orbit around Earth.

As far back as 1971, Hopper talked about one of the goals she had had since childhood. She wanted to go to the stars. She believed that one day when the sun went nova, or blew up, it would destroy the universe as well. People would need to get off the planet Earth and find a new home. According to Billings, she said, "The computer will be man's greatest tool in attaining this new home for mankind." There is no doubt that we couldn't design our spacecraft and carry out our current space missions without the use of advanced computers, just as she foresaw.

The Final Chapter

Going to the stars was a dream Hopper wasn't able to fulfill, along with one other wish—she wanted to live to be ninety-four so she could celebrate the arrival of the new millennium in 2000. She figured that would be the greatest of all New Year's Eve parties.

Sadly, she didn't live to usher in the year 2000. Grace Hopper died in her sleep after a heart attack on New Year's Day, January 1, 1992. She was eighty-six years old.

Admiral Hopper was buried with full military honors at Arlington National Cemetery in Virginia.

This historic cemetery has served as a burial ground since 1864 for soldiers and others who have served in the military or have performed special service in connection with the military. Hopper is well qualified to have her resting place there.

The funeral took place on Tuesday, January 7, 1992. The service began with a navy band playing a hymn. A navy color guard escorted the admiral's casket into the memorial chapel at Fort Myer, where the admiral's flag was draped in black and placed at the front. The navy chaplain read from the Old Testament of the Bible.

The chaplain spoke of Hopper's numerous achievements, of her great love for the navy, and her devotion to serving her country. He spoke of how she encouraged young people to reexamine how things were done to improve them instead of doing things out of habit. When Hopper would leave a meeting, the chaplain recounted, she would often leave with the words, "Fair winds and following seas." An organist played several versions of the beautiful eighteenth-century hymn "Amazing Grace."

The color guard accompanied the casket to the cemetery. The navy band walked in front, as family and friends walked behind it. At the graveside, the

More than a Ship in Port

The USS *Hopper* is an Arleigh Burke–class guided missile destroyer. It was first put into service on January 6, 1996. The USS *Hopper* is 465.9 feet (142 m) long and can travel at more than 31 knots (approximately 35.7 miles per hour, or 57.4 kilometers per hour). It carries a crew of 325. The ship is packed with weapons, electronic warfare systems, and various types of sensors such as radar and sonar.

The ship's motto is *Aude et Effice*, which is Latin for "Dare and Do." This motto was taken as a direct quote from words often used by Rear Admiral Hopper. According to the navy's website, "The phrase captures the spirit of RADM Hopper in her quest for pushing the limits of conventional thinking and looking beyond the norm for innovative solutions and approaches to problem solving."

Or, as Admiral Hopper liked to say, "A ship in port is safe, but that is not what ships are built for."

chaplain read another passage from Scripture. The color guard and band came to attention during a military salute, both an eleven-gun salute from a howitzer battery, which is a type of cannon (for her status as an admiral), and a twenty-one-gun salute for a fallen member of the armed forces.

What She Left Behind

Hopper's legacy lives on in the many contributions she made to computer technology and programs.

This photo, taken in November 2016, shows the crew of the USS *Hopper* in Argentina. The *Hopper*'s mission involved maritime security operations.

She was the inspiration for the Grace Hopper Celebration of Women in Computing, which is an annual conference designed to engage and inform women who have careers in computers. In addition to the Grace Murray Hopper Service Center and the Grace Murray Hopper Center for Computer Learning, there is also the USS *Hopper*, a navy ship named in her honor.

Wise Words

Though Hopper would undoubtedly have been impressed by her namesake ship, bristling with hardware and computers, there is no doubt that the legacy she valued the most was connecting to younger people, especially those between the ages of seventeen and twenty. Dickason reported that Hopper said, "Working with the youth is the most important job I've done. It's also the most rewarding."

In Billings's book, Hopper advised young people not to waste energy coming up with a life plan, but to be prepared to pursue every opportunity they could. That meant they should abstain from smoking, alcohol, and drugs. The reason was that such things damage their brains, and their brains were necessary in order to earn a living.

Hopper was quoted in the April 1985 article "A Living Lady Worthington Descendants Subscriber" as saying, "I like the world of today much better than that a half-century ago. Today the challenges are greater. I like our young people, they know more, they question more, and they learn more. They are the greatest asset this country has."

Though Grace Hopper is gone, her spirit and accomplishments have changed our world. The best way to honor her memory is to live up to her motto: Dare and Do.

Timeline

1906 Grace Murray Hopper is born Grace Brewster Murray on December 9 in New York City.

1924 Grace is accepted into and begins studies at Vassar College.

1928 Hopper graduates from Vassar with a bachelor of arts degree in mathematics and physics. She begins her graduate studies at Yale University.

1930 On June 15, the twenty-three-year-old Grace Murray marries Vincent Foster Hopper.

1934 Hopper receives a PhD in mathematics from Yale University.

1943 Hopper joins the WAVES, a branch of the US Naval Reserve.

1944 In June, Hopper is promoted to the rank of lieutenant (junior grade).

1946 Hopper is released from active duty.

1952 Hopper develops the first computer compiler, called the A-0 System.

1969 Hopper is the first person named Computer Science Man of the Year by the Data Processing Management Association.

1973 Hopper is promoted to the rank of captain. She is also awarded the Legion of Merit that year by Congress for her outstanding service to the military.

1985 Hopper is promoted to rear admiral.

1986 On August 14, at the age of seventy-nine, Grace Hopper retires from the navy for the final time.

1991 Hopper receives the National Medal of Technology—the United States' highest honor in engineering and technology.

1992 On New Year's Day, Hopper suffers a heart attack in her sleep and passes away.

Glossary

algebra A branch of mathematics in which the operations and procedures of addition and multiplication are applied to variables as well as to specific numbers.

binary Consisting of two parts or components; also a mathematical system that uses just two numbers, zero and one, to represent all possible values.

bit Short for "binary digit," the smallest unit of information a computer can process. Bits can have the values 1 (on) or 0 (off).

botany The branch of biological science that deals with the classification and study of plants.

bug A flaw or a problem in a machine, plan, or system.

byte A unit of binary code consisting of eight bits that can be used to represent a single letter or number.

calculus The branch of mathematics used in physics to calculate rates of change and the area and volume of spaces that change.

compiler A computer program that converts other programs from their programming

language version into a form understandable by
computers (called binary code).

data Facts, statistics, or other information.

debug, debugging To remove the flaws or errors
from a machine, program, plan, or system.

digital Computer technology that uses numerical
digits to process information.

geology The study of the physical structure,
composition, and development of the earth or
of rocks.

grant The giving of money for a specific purpose,
such as education.

hymn A devotional song that is sung at a
religious service.

knot The speed at which a ship can travel a nautical
mile (about 1.15 miles) in an hour.

octal A mathematical system that uses eight
numbers, beginning with 0 and ending with 7,
to represent all possible values.

ordnance Cannons, artillery, and all kinds of
military weapons, equipment, and ammunition.

patriotism A feeling of pride, love, and devotion to
one's country.

physics The science that deals with matter and
energy, their properties, and their interactions.

physiology The science that deals with the processes and functions of living organisms and their cells, tissues, and parts.

program A set of steps written in a code understandable to machines that tells a computer how to solve a problem or perform an action.

trigonometry The branch of mathematics that deals with the relations between the sides and angles of triangles.

For More Information

Canadian Coalition of Women in Engineering,
    Science, Trades and Technology (CCWESTT)
c/o Treeline Associates Inc.
1568 Merivale Road, Suite 739
Ottawa, ON K2G 5Y7
Canada
Email: info@ccwestt.org
Website: http://www.ccwestt.org
Facebook and Twitter: @CCWESTT
This nonprofit seeks to bring organizations across
    Canada together to encourage women in STEM
    education and careers.

Expanding Your Horizons Network (EYHN)
5000 MacArthur Boulevard
PMB 9968
Oakland, CA 94613
(510) 277-0190
Website: https://www.eyhn.org
Twitter: @EYHNetwork
The EYHN is a nonprofit organization that
    encourages interest in STEM careers and
    activities for middle and high school girls.

National Center for Women & Information
    Technology (NCWIT)
University of Colorado
Campus Box 417 UCB
Boulder, CO 80309
(303) 735-6671
Email: info@ncwit.org
Website: http://www.ncwit.org
Facebook and Twitter: @ncwit
This nonprofit network of more than eleven
    hundred universities, companies, and
    government organizations works to increase the
    participation of girls and women in computing.

National Women's Hall of Fame
76 Fall Street
PO Box 335
Seneca Falls, NY 13148
(315) 568-8060
Website: https://www.womenofthehall.org
Twitter and Instagram: @WomenoftheHall
This organization honors and celebrates the
    achievements of exceptional American women.
    Its website hosts the biographies of numerous
    celebrated women from the past and present.

Society for Canadian Women in Science and
    Technology
#311 – 525 Seymour St.
Vancouver, BC V6B 3H7
Canada
(604) 893-8657
Website: http://www.scwist.ca
Twitter: @scwist
A nonprofit organization dedicated to promoting
    and empowering girls and women in science,
    engineering, and technology.

Society of Women Engineers
130 East Randolph Street, Suite 3500
Chicago, IL 60611
(312) 596-5223
Email: hq@swe.org
Website: http://societyofwomenengineers.swe.org
Facebook: @SWEorg
Twitter and Instagram: @swetalk
Established in 1950, the SWE is dedicated to
    helping, supporting, and encouraging women in
    engineering fields.

Women's International Center (WIC)
PO Box 880736
San Diego, CA 92168-0736
(619) 295-6446
Website: http://www.wic.org
Facebook: @https://www.facebook.com/Womens
-International-Center-and-Living-Legacy
-Awards-106237102802079
Dedicated to celebrating the accomplishments
of women worldwide, WIC's website offers
biographies of hundreds of important women
creators, workers, and dignitaries.

For Further Reading

Brererton, Catherine. *Women Scientists in Math and Coding.* Mankato, MN: Core Library, 2017.

Goldsmith, Connie. *Women in the Military: From Drill Sergeants to Fighter Pilots.* Minneapolis, MN: Twenty-First Century Books, 2019.

Halligan, Katherine. *HerStory: 50 Women and Girls Who Shook Up the World.* New York, NY: Simon & Schuster Books for Young Readers, 2018.

Hopper, Grace Murray, and Steven L. Mandell. *Understanding Computers.* St. Paul, MN: West Publishing Company, College & School Division, 1990.

McCully, Emily Arnold. *She Did It! 21 Women Who Changed the Way We Think.* Los Angeles, CA: Disney/Hyperion, 2018.

Naber, Therese. *How the Computer Changed History.* Minneapolis, MN: Essential Library, 2016.

Schmermund, Elizabeth. *Women in Technology.* New York, NY: Enslow Publishers, 2017.

Staley, Erin. *Grace Murray Hopper.* New York, NY: Rosen Publishing, 2016.

Swaby, Rachel. *Trailblazers: 33 Women in Science Who Changed the World.* New York, NY: Yearling Books, 2017.

Thimmesh, Catherine, and Melissa Sweet. *Girls Think of Everything: Stories of Ingenious Inventions by Women.* Boston, MA: Houghton Mifflin, 2018.

Wheeler, Jill C., and C. Dianne Martin. *Grace Hopper: Computer Scientist.* Minneapolis, MN: Essential Library, 2018.

Bibliography

"A Living Lady Worthington Descendants Subscriber." *Worthington Descendants Newsletter*, vol. 1, no. 4, April 1985.

Billings, Charlene W. *Grace Hopper: Navy Admiral and Computer Pioneer*. Hillside, NJ: Enslow Publishers, 1989.

Dickason, Elizabeth. "Remembering Grace Murray Hopper: A Legend in Her Own Time." *Chips*, April 1992.

Grace Hopper Celebration. "Grace Hopper Celebration—AnitaB.Org." Retrieved February 7, 2019. https://ghc.anitab.org.

Hamblen, Diane. "Memorial Editorial." *Chips*, April 1992.

Kidwell, Peggy Aldrich. "Stalking the Elusive Computer Bug." *IEEE Annals of the History of Computing*, vol. 20, no. 4, 1998.

Nagler, Gordon R. "Grace Murray Hopper." In *Memorial Tributes*, vol. 6, National Academy of Engineering. Washington, DC: National Academy Press, 1993.

National Women's Hall of Fame. "Hopper, Grace." Retrieved February 7, 2019. https://www.womenofthehall.org/inductee/grace-hopper.

National Women's History Museum. "Grace
    Hopper." Retrieved February 7, 2019. https://
    www.womenshistory.org/education-resources
    /biographies/grace-hopper.
Smithsonian. "Grace Murray Hopper Collection,
    1944–1965." Retrieved April 26, 2019. https://
    www.si.edu/object/siris_arc_140379.
US Navy. "Named for Rear Admiral 'Amazing'
    Grace Hopper." Retrieved February 7, 2019.
    https://www.public.navy.mil/surfor/ddg70
    /Pages/namesake.aspx.

Index